WASPS
Nest Builders

Lynn George

PowerKiDS
press
New York

Published in 2011 by The Rosen Publishing Group, Inc.
29 East 21st Street, New York, NY 10010

First Edition

Editor: Joanne Randolph
Book Design: Kate Laczynski
Photo Researcher: Jessica Gerweck

Photo Credits: Cover, pp. 4, 5, 6, 7, 8 (left), 9, 10–11, 13, 16, 18 (left top corner, bottom), 19, 21 Shutterstock.com; back cover and interior blueprint © www.iStockphoto.com/Branko Miokovic; p. 8 (right) Gay Bumgarner/Getty Images; pp. 12, 20 (right) © Hecker/Sauer/age fotostock; p. 14 (left) © Biosphoto/Borrell Bartomeu/Peter Arnold Inc.; p. 14 (right) © www.iStockphoto.com/Alasdair Thomson; p. 15 © Photoshot/age fotostock; p. 17 © www.iStockphoto.com/Achim Prill; p. 18 (hard hat) © www.iStockphoto.com/Charles Shapiro; p. 18 (top) © www.iStockphoto.com/Vladimir Davydov; p. 20 (left) Gerry Bishop/Visuals Unlimited, Inc./Getty Images; p. 22 Carlos Davila/Getty Images.

Library of Congress Cataloging-in-Publication Data

George, Lynn.
  Wasps : nest builders / Lynn George.
       p. cm. — (Animal architects)
  Includes index.
  ISBN 978-1-4488-0693-5 (library binding) — ISBN 978-1-4488-1347-6 (pbk.) —
ISBN 978-1-4488-1348-3 (6-pack)
  1. Wasps—Juvenile literature. I. Title. II. Series: Animal architects
  QL565.2G45 2011
  595.79—dc22
                                        2010001388

Manufactured in the United States of America

CPSIA Compliance Information: Batch #WS10PK: For Further Information contact Rosen Publishing, New York, New York at 1-800-237-9932

CONTENTS

ALL ABOUT WASPS

What do you think about when you think of a wasp? You may think of a beelike **insect** with a painful **sting**. You may even be scared of them. Wasps are generally helpful bugs, though.

There are many different kinds of wasps. However, all wasps have some

Here a small colony, or group, of wasps begins a nest. Over time the nest will become larger and more wasps will live there.

things that are alike. Each wasp has a head with two **compound eyes**, two **antennae**, and a mouth. Its middle body part, the thorax, has six legs. Most

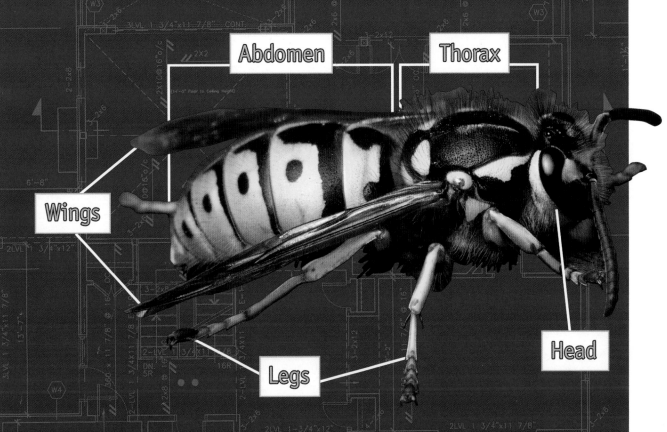

Abdomen

Thorax

Wings

Head

Legs

kinds of wasps also have four wings on the thorax. Wasps can be yellow, red, blue, black, or striped. Wasps live in hot or warm places around the world. They are famous for their nests. Have you ever seen a wasp's nest?

SO MANY KINDS

The female velvet ant has no wings, but the male does have wings. Velvet ants lay their eggs in wasps' or bees' nests. Once the eggs hatch, the young feed on the bees or wasps.

Hornets are the largest kind of social wasp. They are known for having a painful sting.

Would you believe that there are about 20,000 kinds of wasps? It is true! Most kinds of wasps are solitary. This means they spend their lives alone. Females build their nests alone. Young wasps grow up alone, too. Mud daubers and digger wasps are solitary.

Some solitary wasps are parasitic. That means they feed on a **host**. This generally kills the host. Cuckoo wasps are parasitic. Velvet ants, which are hairy wasps, are parasitic as well.

About 1,000 kinds of wasps are social. They live in groups and build large nests. Yellow jackets, hornets, and paper wasps are social.

SWEETS AND MEATS

This wasp is eating nectar from a flower. Wasps help new flowers grow by spreading the flower's pollen, a yellow powder, to other flowers.

A parasitic wasp has laid her eggs on the back of this caterpillar. When the larvae hatch, the caterpillar will be breakfast!

Do you like sweet food? Many adult wasps do. They eat sweet fruits and **nectar** from flowers. Some adult social wasps, such as yellow jackets and European hornets, are known to sometimes eat bugs, too.

Young wasps eat insects and spiders. Adult wasps supply this food in different ways. Solitary wasps put

Some wasps eat fruit, as this one does. It uses its mouthparts to cut through the fruit's skin and then drinks the juice.

prey inside the cells, or rooms, where they lay their eggs. After the eggs **hatch**, the young wasps eat the prey.

Parasitic wasps make sure their young have food when they hatch, too. They lay their eggs on or

inside a living host. The young wasps eat the host after they hatch!

Adult social wasps chew prey to make a paste. They feed the paste to their young. That does not sound like good food to you and me, but young wasps love it!

WHY WASPS NEED NESTS

Wasps use nests to raise their young, just as birds do. Female wasps build nests. The nests have cells for each egg. They lay eggs in the cells in the spring. A wormlike **larva**, or grub, hatches from each egg. The larva eats and grows, then it spins itself a cocoon. Inside the cocoon, it becomes a **pupa**. It breaks

Here you can see some worker wasps raising the young. There are cocoons at the bottom and larvae in the cells above.

out of the cocoon as an adult and leaves the nest.

Social wasps spend only two weeks in their cocoons. They **mate** in the fall, and the males die. Each mated female spends the winter in a safe place. Solitary wasps stay in their cocoons all winter. They come out and mate in the spring.

WHO DOES WHAT IN THE NEST?

Your town has many different jobs to be done, right? A social wasp community does as well. A social wasp nest has three types of wasps. These are the queen, the workers, and the drones. Each kind of wasp has different responsibilities, or jobs to do, in the community.

The wasp at the center of this picture is the queen. There are many workers around her watching over some cocoons. Facing page: This yellow jacket is likely a worker feeding young inside the cells.

The queen's job is to lay eggs. Workers are **undeveloped** females. They do not lay eggs. Instead they make the nest larger, care for the larvae, and guard the nest. Drones are males. Their main job is to mate with queens in the spring, so they can start new nests.

Since solitary wasps do not have big community nests, they do not need workers. There are just queens and drones. They get together only to mate.

HOME ALONE

A potter wasp is placing a live caterpillar into its nest to feed the larva that will hatch. It has stung the caterpillar so that it cannot move.

Some wasps are plant parasites. This seedlike ball goes around a wasp egg. The wasp larva eats the matter inside the ball as it grows into an adult.

Imagine waking up alone in a tiny room with no way out. That is what happens to a solitary wasp. The mother wasp may build a nest with many cells. She may also build many small nests with just one cell in them. She lays an egg in each cell, puts in food, and then seals the cell shut. Some mothers stay to guard their nests from animals that might hurt their larvae. Others leave as soon as they seal up the cells.

The larva in each cell

hatches and grows up alone inside the cell. It does not leave until it becomes an adult. Then it flies away to look for a mate. This is the first time it has seen other wasps!

A GROUP HOME

What would your home be like if hundreds of people lived there? It would be really busy and crowded! That is what the nests of social wasps are like.

A social wasp nest starts small. The queen builds a few cells and lays an egg in each one.

These social wasp workers are making the nest larger. **Facing page:** *Here is a finished paper wasp nest. Generally the nest is used only for one season. Most of the wasp colony dies during the winter.*

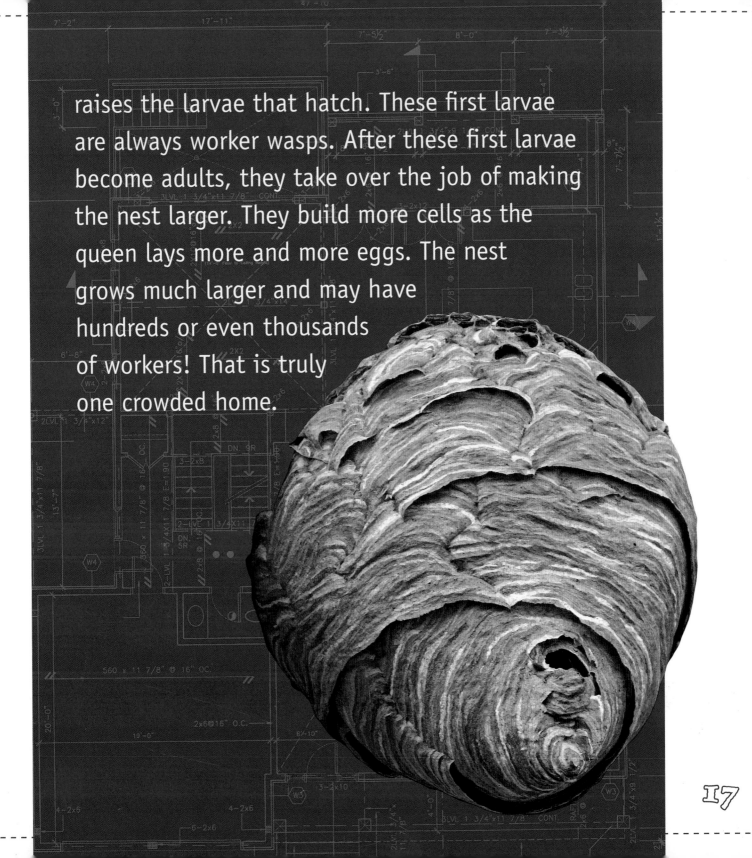

raises the larvae that hatch. These first larvae are always worker wasps. After these first larvae become adults, they take over the job of making the nest larger. They build more cells as the queen lays more and more eggs. The nest grows much larger and may have hundreds or even thousands of workers! That is truly one crowded home.

BUILDING A NEST STEP-BY-STEP

1 Hornets are social wasps that build very large nests. These nests often hang from tree branches. They are shaped somewhat like teardrops and have a single opening at the bottom.

7 In the fall, all the hornets die except for the new queens. The nest will never be used again. Each new queen will start her own nest in the spring.

6 The outer covering keeps the nest safe from enemies and weather. As the nest grows, the workers take paper from the inside and add it to the covering.

2 The queen starts building the nest. She uses a kind of thin, gray paper. To make the paper, she chews up plant matter or wood and mixes it with **saliva.**

3 The queen begins by joining the nest to a branch. She builds cells that are hexagonal, which means they have six sides. She starts in the center and builds outward.

4 Workers take over building the nest. They add more levels below the first one. Each level is joined to the one above by thin **stalks**. There may be eight levels.

5 Each level is called a tier or brood comb. The cells in each comb open on the bottom. Each comb is smaller than the one above it.

19

ALL KINDS OF NESTS

Potter wasp nests look like small clay pots sitting side by side.

The pipe organ wasp shapes mud into balls, which it carries to its nesting place. The wasp uses its mouthparts to make the long tubes where the eggs will be laid.

People build homes of wood, brick, and other matter, right? Wasps build nests of different kinds of matter, too.

As do hornets, many social wasps build paper nests. Most solitary wasps make nests in tunnels under the ground. Others, such as the potter wasp,

make nests out of mud.

How did the potter wasp get its name? A potter is someone who makes pots with clay. That is what a potter wasp does, too. A female wasp mixes water, clay, and saliva. She shapes this mixture into one or more tiny pots. The pots may sit in a row on a small branch or vine. Sometimes potter wasp nests are built on buildings, too.

EVERYONE NEEDS A HOME

All animals, including people, need housing. Shelter keeps animals safe from wind, weather, and predators. Shelter also helps animals keep their babies safe. Some animals use places in nature. They may live in a cave, under a rock, or in a hole in a tree. They do not need any special skills to build their homes.

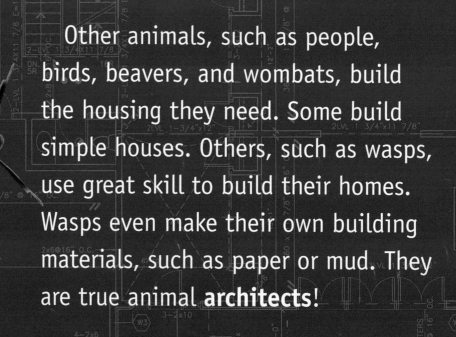

Other animals, such as people, birds, beavers, and wombats, build the housing they need. Some build simple houses. Others, such as wasps, use great skill to build their homes. Wasps even make their own building materials, such as paper or mud. They are true animal **architects**!

GLOSSARY

antennae (an-TEH-nee) Thin, rodlike feelers on the heads of certain animals.

architects (AR-kih-tekts) People who create ideas and plans for a building.

compound eyes (KOM-pownd EYZ) The larger eyes of bugs, which are made up of many simple eyes.

hatch (HACH) To come out of an egg.

host (HOHST) An animal that supplies food for another animal that lives on or in it.

insect (IN-sekt) A small animal that often has six legs and wings.

larva (LAHR-vuh) An insect in the early period of life in which it has a wormlike form.

mate (MAYT) To come together to make babies.

nectar (NEK-tur) A sweet liquid found in flowers.

pupa (PYOO-puh) The second period of life for an insect, in which it changes from a larva to an adult.

saliva (suh-LY-vuh) The liquid in the mouth that starts to break down food and helps food slide down the throat.

stalks (STOKS) Thin parts that are much like the stems of plants and that connect other parts.

sting (STING) Pain caused by an animal using a sharp part to hurt another animal.

undeveloped (un-dih-VEL-upd) Not complete or fully grown.

INDEX

WEB SITES

Due to the changing nature of Internet links, PowerKids Press has developed an online list of Web sites related to the subject of this book. This site is updated regularly. Please use this link to access the list: www.powerkidslinks.com/arch/wasp/